KU-596-095

In libraries throughout Scotland files of local and national newspapers are in daily use to explore the past of the country and of its individual communities. The minor details of everyday life, the routine of local affairs are all there - but so too is the record of the impact of great national and international events. Few events have had a greater impact on Scottish society than the outbreak of the Second World War in 1939. Casualties may have been higher in the 1914-1918 War but what has been described as the 'People's War' was to involve the civilian population in way that this country had not seen before. The front line was to be wherever the bomber could reach. The active participants were not just men in uniform, including the Local Defence Volunteers (later the Home Guard) but the woman in uniform, the civilian in the A.R.P. (Air Raid Precautions) team, the auxiliary fireman, the decontamination squad worker, the nursing auxiliary in the V.A.D. (Voluntary Aid Detachments), and so on. As the extracts show, preparation for the war had begun long before September 1939 - the pace speeding up as the seeming inevitability of war became more and more apparent. Elaborate, and perhaps from the perspective of 1989, unnecessary plans were made for the evacuation of women and children from the main industrial areas and for the distribution of gas masks to the entire civilian population. These two carefully planned and efficiently executed policies reflected the view of the period that 'the bomber would always get through', a view reinforced by the experience of the destruction of Guernica in the Spanish Civil War. There was a widespread expectation that the outbreak of war would see immediate all-out attacks on British towns and cities by a powerful German air force and the probable use of poison gas. For a variety of reasons such all-out attacks did not immediately take place and the first air raid on the United Kingdom occurred six weeks after the outbreak of War. This was, in the event, a not particularly successful attack on Naval vessels in the Firth of Forth, an incident well-described in an extract from the *Dalkeith Advertiser*.

The fifty years that have passed since the events so clearly and vividly described in these newspaper accounts have seen great changes and many of the extracts provide unwitting if graphic evidence of these social changes. One example well illustrates the point - the burgh of Hamilton (population in 1939 39,000) we are told, in the context of an appeal for female volunteer ambulance drivers, had only '267 fully licensed lady drivers'.

Hindsight sometimes perhaps depicts the British people in the Second World War as engaged in a united crusade against the forces of evil and the war as an inevitable historical necessity. As some of our extracts show; there was, before the war, considerable resistance to the prospect of fighting another European war and to the conscription proposals introduced in 1939. After the outbreak of war there was a significant group of conscientious objectors to the war, a group whose views are not always described with sympathy. There was also, as a letter in the *Edinburgh Evening News* suggests, a body of opinion in favour of a negotiated settlement with Germany.

Our extracts range from Aberdeenshire in the North to Peeblesshire in the South, from Dumbarton in the West to Fife in the East. Some stories are universal and can be found in very similar terms in any of the papers of the period, others reflect the particular and local concerns of the area - for example the need for help with the harvest in the agricultural areas of the North East, the efforts to protect the urban population of Glasgow from air raids by strengthening tenement closes with steel beams. The extracts selected cover the great issues of the day - and also some of the more trivial but not less interesting or less characteristic consequences of the war. The closure of cinemas and other places of entertainment at the outbreak of war proved an unpopular and morale damaging decision which, as we show, was soon reversed. The nation soon demonstrated that it could take war in its stride and a vast range of voluntary effort was soon underway - everything from first aid schemes for pet animals injured in air raids and sphagnum moss collecting to dances in aid of the Cigarettes for Soldiers fund.

A main aim of this book is to serve as a resource for schools and notes suggesting some possible uses of the material in this context will be found at the end of the book. However we hope that the book will also interest the adult population -both those who remember the events of 1939, 'doing their bit' and 'digging for victory' and those who only share in the folk memory of these stirring times. A specific use for the book may well be as a trigger for reminiscence groups.

Later in the War – collecting aluminium to build aircraft

Ross

SCOTLAND
1939

EDITED BY
BRIAN D. OSBORNE
&
ROBERT CRAIG

MOTHERWELL
SCOTTISH LIBRARY ASSOCIATION
1989

N E S L S

892759

Handicapped boy being carried on board ship for evacuation overseas

Traffic in Glasgow being warned of gas attack in A.R.P. exercise

940.531
892759

Scottish Library Association
Motherwell Business Centre
Coursington Road
Motherwell

© Scottish Library Association 1989

Newspaper extracts appear by
permission of their publishers

ISBN 0 900649 69 0

Designed by Scott Ballantyne
Photographs supplied by George Outram & Co Ltd
and Falkirk Museum
Typesetting by IPEK, Edinburgh
Printed by Russell Print, Blantyre

An Anderson shelter erected in a Glasgow bedroom

We would like to acknowledge the invaluable help given to the production of this book by colleagues in libraries throughout Scotland who have taken considerable time and trouble to seek out for our selection extracts from their holdings of local newspapers. Anyone who wishes to explore in more depth the events of 1939 and the impact of the coming of war on Scottish society will find in the local studies department of their local public library both a wide range of sources and willing and expert assistance.

Thanks are also due to the newspapers who have kindly agreed to our using extracts for this book. Where these were known all copyright owners have been contacted but in the case of some titles which are no longer published this has not been possible.

The illustrations used throughout Scotland 1939 come from the *Glasgow Herald and Evening Times* Library and we are grateful for permission to use these pictures in this publication.

Finally we would wish to thank Ronald Armstrong, Head Teacher, Ardgowan Primary School, Greenock, for producing the Teachers' Notes which appear at the end of the book. These notes will, we are sure, make this collection of extracts a much more useful educational tool than would otherwise have been the case.

Brian D Osborne
Robert Craig

SCOTLAND 1939

ORDNANCE FACTORY FOR DALMUIR
EMPLOYMENT FOR 1000 MEN

Dalmuir is steadily returning to some of its former activity and the latest announcement that the War Office have decided to establish a Royal Ordnance Factory there is a welcome New Year gift to the burgh of Clydebank. The official intimation states: 'Arrangements have been concluded to take over an existing works, which will be equipped for the manufacture of guns.'

It is expected that when the factory is in full operation it will provide employment for about 1000 men ...

Clydebank Press
13th January 1939

AUXILIARY TERRITORIAL SERVICE
Recruiting Begins in Falkirk

Recruiting for the Auxiliary Territorial Service has now begun in Falkirk ...

Any women between the ages of 18 and 43 who want to serve their country and are not already V.A.D.* or A.R.P.† workers should come to the Drill Hall ...

The Falkirk Company is a General Company attached to the 7th Argyll and Sutherland Highlanders, and, in the event of a national emergency its personnel are allotted various non-combatant duties, clerical and general (i.e. cooks,orderlies, storewomen).

In peace time each volunteer

Forging a 3.7" anti-aircraft gun barrel

must attend at least ten drills a year, and eight days in camp, while in war it is a full-time job, the company may be sent anywhere, and receives pay in the same way as soldiers. The training at drills include elementary drill, anti-gas, first aid, hygiene and Army organisation lectures.

* V.A.Ds. = Voluntary Aid Detachments
† A.R.P. = Air Raid Precautions.

Glasgow Herald
21st January 1939

NEW AIR DEFENCE FOR CLYDESIDE

Glasgow Auxiliary Squadron Converted Into a Fighting Unit

Clydeside's defences against air attack have been materially strengthened by the conversion of the City of Glasgow (Army Cooperation) Squadron, Auxiliary Air Force, into a fighting unit . . . Immediate steps have been taken to re-equip the Glasgow unit with Hawker Hector aircraft - a type used specifically for army cooperation work. . .These aircraft are amongst the fastest fighter biplanes in service at the moment and are capable of a speed of 230 miles per hour.

Glasgow Herald
1st February 1939

AERODROME FOR GRANGEMOUTH
Establishment of Base for Training Reserve Pilots

The Air Ministry have officially

confirmed the report that it has been decided to construct an aerodrome on a site at Grangemouth for the training of Volunteer Reserve pilots from Edinburgh . . .

The new aerodrome, which it is believed will be the largest in Scotland . . . is one of 23 to be established in Britain for the use of the Volunteer Reserve.

Falkirk Herald
4th February 1939

CALL TO NATIONAL SERVICE IN PEEBLESSHIRE
Lord-Lieutenant Outlines Scheme

A clarion call to patriotism was made by Viscount Elibank, Lord Lieutenant of Peeblesshire, when he addressed the first public meeting of the local National Service Committee - and he appealed for widespread support for this voluntary effort.

Progress of the movement up-to-date in Peeblesshire was reported. A notable feature of the units already established was supplied by the A.R.P. scheme of training for wardens. While the number of wardens for Peeblesshire had been officially fixed at 214, the number actually enrolled was 600.

Criticism was again levelled at the War Office for their failure to re-establish a county Territorial unit.

Peeblesshire &
South Midlothian Advertiser
10th February 1939

STORAGE OF FOOD FOR TIME OF EMERGENCY
Mr Johnston Says Masses Unable to Buy Any

Mr Tom Johnston (Stirling and Clackmannan - Lab.) on a Board of Trade Supplementary Vote in which an additional sum of £9000 was asked for for the Food Defence Department said Sir Auckland Geddes* had advised working-class households to prepare a food defence by storing sardines, pilchards and bottles of water . . . He felt disquiet and apprehension that a man who was going to be responsible for feeding the people in a state of emergency should have the effrontery to make proposals of this kind when great masses of people had not the resources to provide themselves with food security for a single weeekend.
* Sir Auckland Campbell Geddes (later Baron Geddes) 1879-1954 - a former cabinet minister was Civil Defence Commissioner for South East England from 1939 -1941.

Glasgow Herald
24th February 1939

BIG JOB FOR A.R.P. WARDENS

Kirkintilloch Police on Friday accepted delivery of 21,000 gas mask containers, and the work of assembling them is likely to be undertaken by the local Wardens. The containers arrived in parcels of 200, flattened out like ordinary cake boxes. It would seem, therefore, that the Wardens are going to be extremely busy, and

outside aid may be sought. In addition to assembling the boxes, 21,000 pieces of special cord will require to be cut to required length, inserted through the 'eyes', and then knotted.

Kirkintilloch Herald
8th March 1939

LARGE SCALE A.R.P. TEST
Cheerful and Efficient Work Despite Conditions

Dalkeith and district played a satisfactory part in the large scale A.R.P. exercises on Monday night. Although robbed of its spectacular value to a great extent owing to the absence of planes and searchlights, cancelled on account of the weather, the test nevertheless provided the authorities with valuable experience . . .

At ten o'clock wailing sirens at various points in the area warned inhabitants of an imminent 'air raid', . . . there was a gratifying response to the request that lights be extinguished. Some time before ten the streets lights were put out, and after the warning had been given, most of the lights in the houses had been obscured . . .

Motorists mostly observed the suggestion that side lights only should be used, but in the all pervading gloom it was surprising to notice how penetrating even these appeared to be . . . .

It was observed that the carriage lights on the London train which passed through Eskbank

shortly after ten o'clock, were screened, and an eerie effect was produced with the thundering noise of the express and only the ruddy glow from the engine cabin racing across the countryside to mark its progress.

Dalkeith Advertiser
30th March 1939

WANTED VOLUNTEERS! KIRKCALDY STILL NEEDS 1340 MORE

Kirkcaldy still needs A.R.P. volunteers . . .

The details are as follows:-

Auxiliary Fire Service -Number required:- 200 men 25-50 years of age required to augment public fire brigade. 60 hours full training as for regular firemen.

Wardens - Number required: - 400 active and dependable men and women over 30 years of age. Duties - Advise fellow citizens near their own residence on the precautions which can be taken in air raids for their protection, and generally act the part of the good neighbour . . .

Rescue and Demolition Parties - Number required:- 70 physically fit men between 25 and 50 years of age, skilled or unskilled, principally drawn from the building trades in the burgh.

First Aid Parties - Number required:- 300 men physically fit, over 30 years of age, with or without first-aid training. Duties - to act as stretcher-bearers . . .

← Evacuee children carrying gas masks in cardboard containers.

Ambulance Drivers and Attendants- Number required:- 150 capable women drivers (not learners) . . .

First Aid Posts - Number required:- 160 capable men and women. Men over 30 years of age, women over 18 years of age Car Owners to Transport Personnel- Number required:- 60 lady owner drivers to transport sitting casualties, administrative officers and staff . . .

Fifeshire Advertiser
1st April 1939

THE 8th ROYAL SCOTS AGAIN
Plans to re-establish the Old Battalion

Peeblesshire will soon have its unit of the 8th Royal Scots again. All the efforts that have been made of late . . . for the re-establishment of the old Battalion have at last succeeded; it is now for the young men of Peeblesshire to show their patriotism by supporting it as their fathers did before them.

As is already known, existing Territorial units are being asked to double their strength and the Territorial authorities . . . have recommended to the War Office that the officers of the 7/9th Royal Scots (The Dandy Ninth) should take in hand to double their strength in the old Eight Battalion area . . .

The 7/9th Royal Scots commenced recruiting last night . . the bands . . . paraded in the

streets during the evening and demonstrations were given of the new Bren gun and anti-tank rifles.

Peeblesshire & South Midlothian Advertiser 21st April 1939

A.R.P. FILM PARADE

A parade comprising a detachment of the 6th Battalion The Cameronians (Scottish Rifles), Royal Engineers, V.A.D.s and members of the W.A.T.S.*, headed by a pipe band, with six motor transport trucks in the rear, marched from Muirhall to the Regal Picture House on Thursday evening to see 'The Warning', a film portraying what might happen in the even of an actual raid on this country.

Members of a decontamination squad in the regulation clothing, with masks and helmets, were standing in the vestibule of the cinema . . .

'The Warning', with its grimly realistic picture of what might happen should Britain be invaded from the air, and displaying impressively the organisation of a city to cope with explosions, gas and fire, ended with a call to national service spoken by Sir John Anderson†. A supplementary appeal was made from the stage by Provost Cassells, who stressed the danger in critical days of delaying until one day it might prove too late.

* W.A.T.S. = Women's Auxiliary Territorial Service
† Sir John Anderson was the cabinet minister

with responsibility for Civil Defence from November 1938. He lent his name to the corrugated iron air raid shelter - the Anderson Shelter. He became Home Secretary in September 1939.

Hamilton Advertiser
22nd April 1939

A.R.P. FIRST AID SERVICES

The large turn out at a meeting in the Bonnyrigg Church Hall on Friday night gave evidence of the keen desire in Bonnyrigg and Lasswade that first aid services in connection with air raid precautions should be available in the burgh. It appears in the Bonnyrigg district at least there is no reluctance to take part in this important branch of A.R.P. work as everyone present at the meeting indicated their willingness to attend classes in order to qualify for the St Andrew's Ambulance Association first aid certificate.

Dalkeith Advertiser
27th April 1939

FLYING RESERVE
Training Centre at Grangemouth

It is announced by the Air Ministry that arrangements have now been completed for the entry of personnel for training at a new Royal Air Force Volunteer Reserve training centre situated at Edinburgh Airport (Grangemouth) . . . Applications for entry as pilots, air observers or wireless operator-air gunners are invited immediately from candidates

resident in the district.

The Royal Air Force Volunteer Reserve has been created in order to ensure the maintenance of adequate reserves of personnel for the reinforcement of the Royal Air Force in times of national emergency and an increase in the strength of the Volunteer Reserve is an important part of the latest expansion scheme.

Falkirk Herald
29th April 1939

R.A.F. Volunteer Reserve Aircraft at Grangemouth [Falkirk Museums]

MILL ARMY ORDERS

Speaking at the A.G.M. of the Roxburgh & Selkirk Unionist Association . . . Lord William Scott, the M.P. for the constituency referred to the recent trial orders placed by the Government with Border mills. He said with the decision to increase the armed forces there would be an

increased need for khaki cloth, and also hosiery, and he hoped that a fair share of these goods would be ordered in the Borders.

Peeblesshire & South Midlothian
Advertiser 12th May 1939

£10,000,000 ORDERS FOR CLYDESIDE

Several big Admiralty contracts are expected to be placed with Clydeside firms before the end of June. The orders now under negotiation represent an aggregate value of almost £10,000,000 and may include a battleship, a cruiser, and several smaller vessels.

Evening Times 5th June 1939

LOCAL MILITIAMEN CALLED TO THE COLOURS

History was made at the weekend . . . For the first time in

history, Britain conscripted some of her man-power for training purposes only. At all other times Britain has actually been at war before considering such a step necessary. . .

Training commenced at once, but every effort was made to let the young men down as lightly as possible till they got used to their new surroundings.

The militiamen are finding the work more pleasant than some of them anticipated. There is little monotony, as the day is divided into periods in much the same manner as a school time-table. Work for the day finishes shortly after 4 o'clock, and from then on the boys may do as they please. Saturday and Wednesday are half holidays . . . .

The War Office announces that seven days' leave are allowed away from the barracks during the six months. At the discretion of the Commanding Officer week-end leave may be granted. Taking things all round, life in the Services is an experience few will regret.

Kirkintilloch Herald
19th July 1939

A.R.P. AMBULANCE SERVICE

While the response to the call for volunteers for this service has had some success, the numbers forward at present cannot be considered satisfactory. Arrangements have now been made to give ladies training in the driving of ambulances, a much

heavier vehicle than most of them have been in the habit of handling. We are informed by the ambulance officer that the trainees who have so far presented themselves have proved very satisfactory and have enjoyed the experience. There are 267 fully licensed lady drivers in the Hamilton area to whom this appeal is made.

Hamilton Advertiser
5th August 1939

NORTH- EAST CALM IN TIME OF CRISIS CITY A.R.P. MEASURES IN ADVANCED STATE

Facing up to the crisis with calm resolution, typical of the North-East, Aberdeen has become, within the short space of a momentous week, completely prepared for sudden emergency.

Although Aberdeen is classed as a neutral area, defence measures in the city and preparations - if the worst come to the worst - for a 'black-out' have reached their present peak of efficiency, thanks to the admirable co-operation of civilians and A.R.P. authorities. . .

Steps have been taken to safeguard the General Post Office and Telephone House buildings . . . The fifty most valuable pictures in the Art Gallery have been marked with coloured discs and, at the first sign of danger, they will be rapidly removed from the walls and stacked away in a

secure hiding place which has been prepared for them.

Equipment was sent out on Tuesday for light and heavy rescue parties and road repair squads. The supplies, consisting of steel helmets, protective clothing, respirators and rubber boots, have been sent to the Corporation Workshops.

BOY SCOUTS' PART

Aberdeen Boy Scouts, of fifteen years or over, who wish to volunteer for orderly service in the event of a national emergency, are asked to report to headquarters as soon as possible.

'The Scout movement locally has already been asked to supply the services of certain orderlies who could be attached to the local coast-watching headquarters,' states Dr W Douglas Simpson, hon. county secretary of the movement. In the event of an emergency, he said there would be a considerable number of such demands for various other kinds of service as was the case during the last war.

Aberdeen Bon-Accord and
Northern Pictorial
31st August 1939

CLYDE SHIPYARD WORKERS

Workers in the Clyde shipyards and engineering establishments have received permission to work all overtime required.

Inspecting a gun barrel in a Scottish ordnance factory

The permission has been reached following a conference between the Confederation of Shipbuilding and Engineering Unions (Clyde District Committee), the Clyde Shipbuilders Association and the North-West Engineering Trades Employers Association. . . it was agreed that the national overtime and night shift agreement be suspended . . . and that the men be permitted to work all the overtime required by the firms. Formerly this was restricted to thirty hours a month.

Lennox Herald
25th September 1939

CONSCRIPTION PLAN
Labour Party's Reasons for Opposition: Falkirk Meeting

Reasons for the opposition of the Labour Party to the proposed introduction of conscription in Great Britain were outlined by Mr Tom Johnston, M.P. for West Stirlingshire, a former Lord Privy Seal, when he addressed a crowded meeting in Falkirk Town Hall on Sunday evening. . .

Mr Johnston said. . . he would. . . like to know what the people were to be conscripted for. Was it to prevent Italy getting Jibuti from the French. . . . He did not think the people of this country should be conscripted to prevent the return of Togoland to Germany. There was . . . a very grave danger that conscription would be used to defeat progressive forces in the country. In France, where conscription was in force, the ruling Government, when they were in danger of defeat on certain issues, had called certain classes of men to the colours, and had thereby deprived them of their civilian rights. The same tactics, which were the negation of democracy, could be introduced in this country.

Falkirk Herald 1st April 1939

MINISTERS AT PRESBYTERY REFUSE HELP NATIONAL SERVICE: Say are Pacifist

Four ministers of Kirkcaldy Presbytery have refused to have anything to do with a proposal to co-operate in National Service work.

Kirkcaldy Presbytery on Tuesday agreed to form a Church and National Service Committee . . .

'I wish to dissociate myself from this decision on the grounds that, firstly I am a pacifist, and, secondly, that no action of comparable magnitude has been taken through the courts of the Church to further peace conferences when these have been held, or to protest against the arms programme pursued by our own Government.'

This remark of the Rev. Robert Murray came when the Presbytery agreed to form a committee . . .

Fifeshire Advertiser 8th April 1939

CONSCRIPTION
'Emphatic Protest' at Falkirk 'Attack on Freedom'

Protests against the introduction of conscription were made at a meeting held in the Union Halls, Graham's Road, Falkirk on Wednesday evening. . .

Councillor Hamilton also criticised conscription on the ground that it made no contribution to the defences of the country. Conscript soldiers were not good soldiers. They had no zest for the tasks they were called on to perform. Conscription would upset the economic life of the country. It would cause untold hardship in the homes of the working-class families.

Baillie Strachan stressed the point that the introduction of conscription was a glaring violation of the election pledges of the Government and of the personal pledges given by the Prime Minister.

The following resolution was submitted to the meeting and unanimously adopted 'That this mass meeting of Falkirk citizens records its emphatic protest against the Chamberlain government introducing conscription. This, in their opinion is a violation of the election pledges given given by the present Government and is the first step towards the complete destruction of the freedom of the British people. They further would urge H.M. Government immediately to enter into a mutual pact with Soviet Russia for the defence of the peace of the world.'

Falkirk Herald 6th May 1939

CLYDEBANK YOUTH REPRESENTED ON DEPUTATIONS TO PARLIAMENT

In view of the recent high feeling of youth on the introduction of the Military Training Bill I was elected by the National Youth Campaign as a delegate representing the youth of Clydebank on a deputation of youth from all parts of Britain to the House of Commons, writes John S. McCafferty, of the local Emergency Committee. . .

. . .on entering the lobby of the House of Commons I saw fifty fellow-delegates representing as many industrial centres in England and Scotland. All seemed actively engaged either in conversation with their respective M.P.'s or in last minute scrutiny of their notes. This was to me a most inspiring and heartening sight, fully illustrative of the determination of British youth to defy any introduction of pro-fascist policies or compulsory training, military or industrial . . ..

With surprisingly little delay Mr David Kirkwood* received me and we had a very enlightening discussion . . .

He expressed his pleasure and delight in the fact that the youth of Clydebank were putting their burgh on the no Conscription map. He also contended that he would work untiringly to defeat the Conscription Bill even to the extent of protest strikes on the

Clydeside . . . .

* David Kirkwood (1872 - 1955) Labour M.P. for Dumbarton Burghs (later East Dumbartonshire) from 1922 - 1951. Created 1st Baron Kirkwood 1951.

Clydebank Press 19th May 1939

THE EDITOR'S POST BAG
At the Eleventh Hour

'Professor' writes: I should like to add my plea . . . for an immediate armistice pending an international conference to attempt to settle the present problems of Europe by peaceful means. This is the eleventh hour but there is yet time to prevent the holocaust and disaster that is the only certain result of war on a modern scale.

Though our first reaction to Hitler's proposals is to reject them indignantly after what has recently occurred in Poland, yet reflection will show that nothing is to be gained from this attitude. Do not let our aversion to Nazism and all it stands for blind us to the fact that only by such a conference can we hope to reach a lasting solution of the present

international problems. In Hitler's desire for some neutral country to act as mediator, we see, at last, the understanding that his word alone is worthless.

Edinburgh Evening News
12th October 1939

WOULD NOT EVEN CLOTHE TROOPS

J.H. Kennedy, 21 year old hosiery machinist of Blackwood Street, Barrhead, would resign from his job if he thought the garments he helped to make were for the troops. He said so yesterday when with fourteen other conscientious objectors he applied for military exemption at the first Military Training Tribunal held in Glasgow. His application was granted unconditionally.

Scottish Daily Express
17th October 1939

CONCHIE* SAYS 'I WOULD ONLY PRAY'

J.A. Murray, 21 year-old conscientious objector of . . . Maryhill, Glasgow told the Military Tribunal in Glasgow yesterday that if the country were threatened with destruction he would not lift a finger to save it. Instead, he would pray for 'the removal of the spirit of war'. His application for exemption from military service was rejected unconditionally.

*'Conchie' - slang term for conscientious objector

Scottish Daily Express
19th October 1939

A bomb proof shelter for works machinery

SOURCE OF LOCAL TROUBLES
Foreign Situation to Blame
Prospective Glasgow
Candidate's Views

'Local troubles such as rates and rent wars, inactivity of the shipbuilding and other heavy industries and the question of the unemployed can all be boiled down to one source, the international situation,' said Flight-Lieutenant Hugh Black, prospective Unionist candidate for the Tradeston Division of Glasgow . . . 'The most disheartening thing to my mind is the way some of our best brains and skilled labour is being employed in unproductive work such as A.R.P. and re-armament contracts.'

Glasgow Herald
24th January 1939

GERMAN REFUGEES

About fifty applications weekly are received from people in Germany anxious to come to Scotland according to a bulletin launched by the Scottish Christian Council for Refugees which was inaugurated last December to aid the 'non Aryan'* Christian refugees from Germany and Central Europe.

Permits were obtained for 103 men women and children from Prague. . . Between 20 and 30, mostly men, are awaiting the permission of the Gestapo† to leave the country.

*Nazi theory divided races into Aryan and non-Aryan. Jews, Slavs, Poles, Serbs, etc.

were categorised as non-Aryan.
†Gestapo = German secret police.

Motherwell Times
31st March 1939

HITLER VICTIMS

The plight of thousands of people in Europe is brought vividly home to residents in the peaceful Borderland by the arrival of another batch of refugees at . . . Selkirk. . . . One young girl is a Pole who had to flee from Prague when Hitler's hordes marched in. Only receiving an hour in which to pack, many left their treasured belongings behind, not even stopping long enough to raise some money. . . . Many of their men-folk are in concentration camps and it seems that they might never see each other again.

Peeblesshire & South Midlothian Advertiser
7th April 1939

BONNYRIGG ICE CREAM MERCHANT AT COURT
SLOGAN CAUSES ITALIAN ANNOYANCE
ANIMOSITY IN DISTRICT

The sequel to a dispute between two ice cream merchants, one an Italian at Bonnyrigg, was heard at the Edinburgh Sheriff Court on Saturday. A slogan 'Why support the Axis?* Show your patriotism. Buy British!' appeared to have caused the trouble. The Italian erased his rival's slogan with green paint.

John Riccoboni, ice cream merchant . . . admitted that on June 27 in Hopefield Place, Bonnyrigg, he maliciously damaged the lettering on the side of the motor van by painting over the lettering.

An agent on accused's behalf said 'Evidently for some time past these slogans have been responsible for a certain amount of animosity in Bonnyrigg district.'

*Axis. The alliance between Nazi Germany and Fascist Italy.

Dalkeith Advertiser
13th July 1939

BRITONS LEAVE POLAND AND REICH

While Germany's 'trial mobilisation' is making rapid progress - it stated that by tonight she will have 2,000,000 men under arms - Britons have been advised to leave Poland.

Evening Times
22nd August 1939

ALIENS RUSH TO REGISTER

Hundreds of aliens resident in Glasgow called on Monday at the Aliens Department, Glasgow Police Headquarters, to register under the new Aliens Order. A large number queued up outside the building, while others were seated inside the premises waiting their turn to register.

Kirkintilloch Herald
6th September 1939

The Hudson ARP shelter demonstrated in Glasgow April 1939.

'THIS MAN' HITLER

Germany under Hitlerism has acquired the unenviable distinction of being one of the most unenlightened nations in the world. Culturally it has become a Dark Continent. Its literature is decadent, if not dead. Its most brilliant scientists have been thrown into concentration camps or driven into poverty stricken exile. . . .its universities, the inheritors of great names and illustrious traditions, are now little more than propaganda schools in which sound learning is despised. Many of its churches are no longer Christian institutions but temples of pagan worship, where the state is glorified and the Fuhrer made the supreme object of devotion. The old Germany is dead. Adolf Hitler has killed it.

Aberdeen Bon-Accord and Northern Pictorial 7th September 1939

GERMANY INTERNALLY WEAK, SAYS WOMAN

'My impression is that Germany is internally weak, and that second thoughts about the Russian pact will not ease the situation . . .' This is the opinion of a young Edinburgh woman . . . who has just returned from Germany to the city.

'Go at once or we will treat you as we have treated the Jewish women.' That was the 'farewell' given by a German officer to her in a library in Munich last Saturday week, and the young woman told a reporter in an interview, she took the hint and caught a train an hour later across the Swiss frontier. Informed by the common German police that there would be no war with Britain, she waited in Switzerland until she, at the last moment, managed to make the journey home this weekend.

Aberdeen Weekly Journal 7th September 1939

'AXIS' AT KEITH

David and Mary Sorrie piloted donkeys named 'Hitler' and 'Mussolini' respectively into the lead at Keith Show. It was another coup for the 'axis', (not without 'strafing').

Aberdeen Bon-Accord and Northern Pictorial 10th August 1939

DAMAGE TO ITALIAN'S SHOPS

John Doyle . . . was charged at the Burgh Court with committing a breach of the peace outside the shops of Antonio Coia . . . and Guiseppi Ferri . . . on Saturday night, in both of which windows were broken although Boyle was not charged with these acts. It was stated that about 9.30 p.m. Doyle approached Coia's shop shouting out his 'hate' of Italian Fascisti ....'s and his wish for a bomb. He went away and behaved in the same fashion in Ferri's shop . . . Later the window of Coia's shop was broken and Doyle was outside shouting epithets about Italians.

Police Judge Patterson - 'It can't be allowed, especially in these trying times. If these people are conducting business in a fair legal way they should not be molested, irrespective of their nationality.' He imposed a fine of £1 or 10 days.

Hamilton Advertiser 16th September 1939

Evacuees board train at Ibrox

PROTECTION OF GLASGOW
Provision of Balloon Barrage

Air Marshal Boyd is to visit Glasgow to discuss with the military and civil authorities preliminary arrangements for the organisation of the Glasgow barrage. . . The scheme was to have a squadron of 50 balloons for Glasgow requiring a trained personnel of 550 officers and men.

Glasgow Herald
10th January 1939

EVACUATING CHILDREN

Sir,

Having had occasion to visit a town in the Upper Ward of Lanarkshire recently, I was amused and also annoyed at the attitude of a large number of the women towards the Government scheme of evacuating children in the event of war. The maiden ladies, of whom there is an over abundance, are the worst offenders. This is the sort of thing one continually hears - 'Isn't it dreadful? Fancy having to take in slum children.' 'Yes, it's terrible, our houses will be ruined.' 'We will have to lift our carpets.' 'I will certainly put away my down quilts and good linen.' I'm afraid my sympathy is with the children who might have to enter such homes.

What the reaction would be if the fathers of the said children refused to fight or engage in any war work one can easily imagine. The hands of these poor defenceless women would go up in horror and with one voice they would wail -'What's to become of us?' I for one would be tempted to say -'Wrap yourselves up in your carpets and hibernate beneath your down quilts until such peaceful times as when there will be no children left to dirty carpets or take the polish off floors and furniture.'

ONE WILLING TO SERVE
Hamilton Advertiser
11th February 1939

BURGH AS 'STAND STILL' AREA IN WARTIME

Addressing the meeting of the Trades and Labour Council on the burgh's Air Raid Precautions the Hon. Treasurer remarked that Motherwell and Wishaw was regarded by the Government as a vulnerable area in the event of enemy air raids.

It was estimated that the city of Edinburgh would carry a percentage of 80 per cent risk in comparison with London's 100 per cent. The percentage estimated for Motherwell and Wishaw was 60.

It was not proposed to evacuate women and children from the burgh in war-time. 'We would neither send any of our civilian population outside nor would we receive people from other areas - we were to be what is known as a 'stand-still' area.

*Motherwell Times
28th April 1939*

GREENOCK WILL TAKE TO THE HILLS IF WAR COMES
Labour Opposition to A.R.P. Priority Proposal

When you ask the majority the people what they are going do if war comes to Greenock th will tell you they are going to d nothing regarding A.R.P. shelter: but are going to take to the hill: This statement was made by Mr McArthur, a Labour Member, at meeting of Greenock Corporatio

Evening Times 16th May 1!

GOVERNMENT EVACUATION SCHEME
PLANS FOR DALKEITH

Dalkeith . . . is to be a reception area for children and others evacuated from Edinburg A number of householders in th burgh have offered to take and care for children who are not accompanied by their mothers. This valuable piece of National Service has been recognised by the issue to these householders of a window card, along with a letter of thanks from the Secretary of State for Scotland. . . . Any householders who have surplus rooms according to the government standard are urged to volunteer to receive children if they have not already done so.

Board and lodging for such children will be paid at the rate of 10/6* per week when only one child is taken, 8/6 per week per child when more than one child is taken.

* 10/6 £0.52p.; 8/6 = £0.42p.

*Dalkeith Advertiser
24th August 1939*

A.R.P. shelters, Edinburgh August 1939

CLOSES MADE SAFER TODAY
Steel struts arrive

Steel struts for the reinforcement of tenement closes to turn them into air-raid shelters will arrive in Glasgow this morning. Material sufficient for 20,000 tenements is to be provided.

*Scottish Daily Express
1st September 1939*

PEEBLESSHIRE AND THE CRISIS
Defensive Plans Well Forward

In Peeblesshire, as in all other parts of the country in these days of crisis, there has been great activity in the various spheres engaged in the preparation of defensive measures. . .

The County Road Staff have had many extra duties thrown on them . . . the pavements at street corners were all marked off in white in case a black-out became necessary. Workmen have been busy converting the Public Baths at Peebles for use as a first- aid post in connection with the A.R.P. scheme. At the County Roads depot . . . a start has been made

Black-out precautions – painting white
stripes on trees in Aberdeen

with the erection of decontamination quarters.

Evacuation from from Edinburgh into the Peeblesshire evacuation area is in progress today, following upon the BBC announcement on Thursday.

Peeblesshire & South Midlothian Advertiser 1st September 1939

GLASGOW DEFENCE COMPLETE

Glasgow's organisation for defence against air attack has now been completed. . . . The work of safeguarding tenements and reinforcing closes is being tackled vigorously; trenches are being dug in the public parks and police officers are patrolling the streets, carrying their steel helmets and gas masks.

Glasgow Evening News 2nd September 1939

INFIRMARY EVACUATION
Patients Removed Home Or To Other Hospitals

In accordance with an instruction received from the Department of Health, evacuation of patients from Falkirk and District Royal Infirmary was recently proceeded with on a gradual scale and completed on Thursday.

Patients whose condition was such that they could not be taken to their homes were conveyed by ambulances to hospitals in less vulnerable areas. The less serious cases were taken home either by ambulance or private car. The work of evacuation proceeded smoothly, and with an entire absence of any excitement or suggestion of panic.

The matron and staff are now standing by to undertake what duties a state of emergency may require of them.

Falkirk Herald 2nd September 1939

DUMBARTON PREPARED
Obscuring 'Dumbarton'

A Government order is that in national emergency all lettering on business or other premises which can be read from the air and so be likely to reveal the identity of a town to enemy aircraft must be obliterated.

It is only recently that Messrs. Hiram Walker & Son Ltd. completed one of their huge storage buildings by having the word 'Dumbarton' painted in monster letters with 'Distillery' in smaller letters below . . . We understand that steps will be taken by the firm to have the sign obliterated in some manner if the necessity for so doing arises.

Lennox Herald
2nd September 1939

FOUNDRY HORNS 'FADE AWAY' SIRENS, HOOTERS NOW PROHIBITED

The voice of the factory siren or hooter will no longer be heard throughout the land except when required to give warning of air raids.

On Friday instructions were sent to local authorities to put the air raid warning system into full operation.

Kirkintilloch Herald
6th September 1939

EVACUATION IN DALKEITH
By One of the Workers

Dalkeith had its part in the great work of receiving the evacuated children and mothers who left Edinburgh on Friday and Saturday. The number received (over 400) was much smaller than the maximum for which the Burgh was required to prepare. But the staff of workers showed what they could do by the thoroughness of their preparation and the efficiency and kindness with which they did their job.

The first arrivals reached the Corn Exchange by bus about half-past ten . . . At the Corn Exchange they were given a cup of soup and assigned to their billets by the Billeting Officers and conducted there by Billeting Assistants.

They found in most cases a hearty welcome in houses both large and small, and many stories are being told of happy responses to the efforts to make them feel at home. It was only natural that the children should be somewhat timid at this sudden change to a strange place. But the truth is that many a housewife was just as fearful as any child at the thought of taking in newcomers she had never seen before. On both sides the first forebodings were quickly overcome, and friendly contacts established. It is true, of course, that some were house-sick and mother-sick, like the little chap who said 'It doesn't matter how many toys you give me, it's my mummy I want.'

Dalkeith Advertiser
7th September 1939

ADVERTISEMENT
MUSSELBURGH & FISHERROW CO-OPERATIVE SOCIETY LTD

Gas Mask Containers
    Suedette, White, Blue, Red 1/6*
    Waterproof Cloth 1/9
    Brown Canvas 2/-
    Fibre Case 2/3
(Fancy Check Material. Assorted Designs to match any Outfit
    Leather Cloth 3/-
(Assorted Colours. Smart New Style)
* 1/6 = £0.07 3/- = 0.15

Dalkeith Advertiser
12th October 1939

TWO GLASGOW TUNNEL AIR RAID SHELTERS

A start is at last to be made with Glasgow's much talked-of tunnel shelter in the Springburn district. The tunnel, which will be the first public underground shelter to be constructed in Scotland, will be made by excavating into the hillside at Carron Street. . . Another underground shelter with accommodation for 700 persons is to be constructed off the Gallowgate in the railway tunnel under the site of the old barracks.

Evening News
22nd November 1939

Shop windows taped to stop flying glass in event of an air raid. Glasgow September 1939.

WEDDING POSTPONED

The wedding which was to have taken place at Banchory on Friday between Squadron-Leader Vernon Dillon Moreshead, Royal Air Force, and Miss Violet Kerr, Invery, Banchory, has been postponed owing to the international situation.

Aberdeen Bon-Accord and
Northern Pictorial
31st August 1939

PUBLISHERS' NOTE

The 'Peeblesshire Advertiser' and 'South Midlothian Advertiser' are issued to-day in reduced size, but with a full service of local news.

This has been rendered necessary by army mobilisation of half of our staff at such short notice that it has been impossible to replace them in time.

THE LIBRARIAN

Mr W E Macpherson, the Burgh Librarian, has been called away on national service and Miss Bethune, his assistant, has been in charge of the library.

NO PICTURES

Perhaps the main grouse that has been heard in Peebles this week is that the picture houses have been closed. The public may not have long to wait ere this form of entertainment will again be made available to them.

Peeblesshire & South Midlothian Advertiser 8th September 1939

MANY ABERDEEN PEOPLE WERE ON BOARD TORPEDOED LINER ATHENIA

More than a score of passengers from Aberdeen were on board the Athenia when the liner was torpedoed. They are natives of the city returning to their homes in Canada and United States.

All of them, with the exception of one man, were women and children. Several of them were mothers taking their families home.

ABERDEEN WOMAN'S GRAPHIC STORY

'I was sitting with my cousin and her little daughter when the torpedo struck the ship,' said Miss Smith when she arrived home. 'I knew right away what had happened. Everybody must have known.

The three of us made a dash for the deck, but in the confusion we became separated. I had just got on deck when the lifeboats were being lowered. Then another torpedo hit the Athenia.

Everybody was wonderfully calm under the circumstances, and the ship's officers marshalled the people quietly and efficiently

into the lifeboats. . . We were lowered into the water in the boat, and when I looked out across the sea I saw the submarine rise to the surface. It fired a shot across the wireless mast but failed to hit it.'

The Donaldson Line passenger liner 'Athenia' sailing from the Clyde was torpedoed without warning on 3rd September by the German submarine U30. She sank with the loss of 112 lives.

Aberdeen Journal 7th September 1939

INVERNESS CHURCH SERVICES IN AFTERNOON

Inverness Presbytery decided at a meeting on Inverness on Tuesday to suggest to Kirk Sessions that the normal evening service should be held in the afternoon to make artificial lighting unnecessary.

Aberdeen Journal 7th September 1939

VALE OF LEVEN SHELTERS AND TRENCHES

Plans for the provision of air raid shelters at Port- Glasgow, Gourock, Alexandria, Renton, Bonhill and Balloch were approved within a period of 24 hours. Within the same period plans for a control room at Clydebank were authorised.

These facts were stated on Monday by Sir Cecil M. Weir, District Commissioner for Civil Defence in the West of Scotland...

'We are very pleased to note

that the people are today carrying their gas masks with them,' said Sir Cecil. 'It is a habit that should be acquired very quickly. It is quite evident that a nation that could torpedo the Athenia would have no hesitation in using other methods of warfare.'

Lennox Herald 9th September 1939

PIGEON SERVICE

Owing to the crisis all pigeon racing has been cancelled and several Scottish Federations have failed to complete their young bird programme. Mr A.N. Hutton . . . has been appointed general organising officer for Scotland. Many months ago Government officials approached Mr Hutton to accept this important post in case of Britain going to war, when pigeons would be required for all fighting services to carry messages when all other means of communication had failed. The War Office have selected Scotland's most capable official to carry through this important work. Fanciers should now wait for

Collecting scrap metal for war work

instructions from the General Officer.

Hamilton Advertiser
9th September 1939

STONEHOUSE
Rex Cinema

It will be of interest to supporters of the flicks* to note that the times have been altered to suit emergency conditions. As and from Thursday, 14th September, the programme will be a continuous one, commencing at 5 o'clock instead of 6.15 as formerly. For the children a matinee will be run every Saturday, commencing at 2 p.m. A splendid series of first-class pictures have been booked for some time to come and patrons can rest assured of real star entertainment.

* 'flicks' = contemporary slang for cinema films

Hamilton Advertiser
16th September 1939

FIRST AID FOR RAID-INJURED PETS

A scheme to provide first-aid for small animals should an air-raid occur is being arranged in Aberdeen.

Collecting centres are being selected for injured cats and dogs. Inspectors of the Aberdeen Association for the Prevention of Cruelty to Animals will give advice at these centres as to which animals should be destroyed.

Volunteers, for whom the Association are appealing, will take less badly injured animals to the Cats' and Dogs' Home where treatment will be given by members of the veterinary profession.

So that their dogs may be returned after an air raid owners should see that their names and addresses are on their collars. It is important also to have a muzzle and strong chain for use in an emergency.

Aberdeen Weekly Journal
21st September 1939

RAID ON LORRIES

Many heavy lorries belonging to Peeblesshire coal merchants and contractors have been commandeered for national service these past few days. In not a few instances severe inconvenience has been caused the owners of vehicles, but the necessities of war come first, and like many others whose routine has been severely upset, they have just had to grin and bear it.

Peeblesshire & South Midlothian Advertiser
22nd September 1939

NATIONAL REGISTRATION
All Must Register on Friday

Every man, woman and child (except members of the Forces) in Great Britain and Northern Ireland, on Friday night, September 29, will be entered in Britain's war-time 'Domesday Book'. Commercial travellers journeying by train through the night; tramps trudging from one casual ward to another; air raid wardens and firemen at their posts - all will have to complete the Registration form. . .

As local registrar, Mr James Frame will be responsible for carrying out the work in the registration district of Hamilton . . .

The area has been divided into 63 registration districts. Enumerators - one for each district - were appointed some time ago, and have since been standing by ready to begin their tasks as soon as the scheme was brought into operation.

The return on the schedule will be used not only for national registration but also for the purpose of food rationing. It is in the interest of every householder, therefore, as well as being his or her public duty, to fill up the schedule carefully and accurately.

Hamilton Advertiser
23rd September 1939

DUMBARTON-BUILT SHIPS HELD UP

Fifty-three intending passengers by mailboat from Holyhead to Ireland waited in vain all day on Tuesday for the L.M.S vessel Cambria (3462 tons), registered in Dublin, to sail. . .

The crews of the Cambria and of two L.M.S.* cargo boats registered in Dublin . . . all three Dumbarton-built - had refused to sail under the Eire flag, putting forward the argument that no compensation would be payable if they were attacked by the enemy under that flag.

'We are sorry that we have inconvenienced passengers,' said a member of the Cambria crew to a reporter, 'yet we know that they support us in our case. We are

← Policeman in gasmask check identity cards.

British sailors and entitled to sail under the British flag.'
*L.M.S. = London, Midland & Scottish Railway Company

Lennox Herald
23rd September 1939

WAR-TIME HINTS AND WARNINGS

Cheap rates for long-distance telephone calls have been done away with. The lines have to be kept free for urgent calls dealing with national defence.

Sew a name and address label on to your children's clothing so that they cannot pull it off.

Cyclists or pedestrians who stand chatting off the kerb after dark run the risk of being knocked down by an invisible car.

Hamilton Advertiser
30th September 1939

BLACK-OUT FAULTS

Windows insufficiently darkened over the whole surface.

Windows showing light owing to badly fitted blinds or curtains

Rooms being entered and lights thoughtlessly or wilfully switched on prior to drawing blinds or adjusting curtains.

Entering into unblinded rooms with lights or flashing torches.

Allowing lights from a room or hall to stream into adjoining unblinded rooms.

Permitting curtains and blinds to blow back and thus allow beams of light to escape at

intervals.
Lennox Herald 7th October 1939

SUMMER TIME EXTENDED

The Government proposes that Summer Time this year should be extended until the night of November 18-19 . . .

It is learned that this decision has been reached by the Government in consultation with the French Government . . .

The normal date on which Summer Time was to end was October 8. Extension has been urged in several quarters to ease the difficulties of the black-out arrangements.
Lennox Herald 7th October 1939

LORD PROVOST ASKED TO RE-OPEN SCHOOLS

A deputation of Govan housewives . . . called on Lord Provost Dollan at Glasgow City Chambers yesterday and demanded the immediate opening of the city schools. They stated that children were running wild and becoming demoralised owing to the lack of educational discipline.

Scottish Daily Express
10th October 1939

FALSE AIR RAID SIGNAL

Inhabitants of Dumbarton got quite a scare about 7.30 on Tuesday evening when, for the first time since the war started, a sound no one desired to hear was carried over the town . . . There was considerable excitement . . . until it was realised that the sound, given out by one of the public works' syrens due to a technical fault, was the 'Raiders Passed' signal.

The air raid warning is a warbling, or fluctuating note of two minutes duration. The 'Raiders Passed' signal is a continuous blast of two minutes duration.

Lennox Herald
14th October 1939

MORE LIGHT OR WE STOP AT 8 p.m. SAY TRAM MEN

Glasgow's 4000 municipal transport men have unanimously decided to remove their trams and buses from the streets at eight o'clock nightly as from next Thursday unless better lighting is permitted on their vehicles.

Scottish Daily Express
14th October 1939

BOMBING RAID ON THE FORTH ENEMY PLANES OVER DALKEITH AND DISTRICT
Exciting Air Fights Witnessed

Aerial activity over Dalkeith and district on Monday afternoon created many rumours and much speculation before it was officially announced in the evening that German bombers had carried out a daring daylight raid on warships in the Firth of Forth.

It was while they were being attacked and driven off from their objective that the enemy planes, with British fighting machines in hot pursuit, became visible to many perplexed people in this district. The movements of the planes were watched with interest, but little alarm, and as no warning sirens had sounded, it was generally concluded at first that practice operations were taking place. The machine-gun firing, however, became too realistic for this explanation to be convincing, and with anti- aircraft firing also being heard, it was gradually realised that the planes were engaged in serious business. . . It seemed almost incredible that the people of Dalkeith and district should be having such a close up view of the first enemy air attack on Britain in this war.

In a joint communiqué issued by the Admiralty, the Air Ministry and the Ministry of Home Security . . . it was stated 'To-day, October 16th between 9 a.m. and 1.30 p.m., several German aircraft reconnoitred Rosyth*. This afternoon, about half-past two, a series of bombing raids began. These were directed at the ships lying in the Forth, and were conducted by about a dozen machines.

All the batteries opened fire upon the raiders, and the Royal Air Force fighter squadron ascended to engage them.

No serious damage was done

to any of His Majesty's ships. One bomb glanced off the cruiser Southampton, causing slight damage near her bow, and and sank the Admiral's barge and pinnace which were moored empty alongside . . .

On the other hand, four bombers at least out of the twelve or fourteen were brought down, three of them by fighters of the R.A.F.

The first contact . . . took place off May Island at the entrance to the Firth of Forth at 2.35 p.m. when two enemy aircraft were intercepted. They were driven down by our aircraft from 4000ft. to within a few feet of the water, and chased out to sea.

Another enemy aircraft was engaged ten minutes later over Dalkeith. It fell in flames into the sea.

* Rosyth. Important naval base near Dunfermline on the North side of the Firth of Forth.

Dalkeith Advertiser
19th October 1939

VICTIMS OF ROYAL OAK SINKING
Ordinary Seaman Edward H Barker

Another victim of the U-boat attack on H.M.S. Royal Oak was Ordinary Seaman Edward H Barker, the eldest son of Mr & Mrs David Barker, Binniehill, Slamannan, who have a family of five girls and three sons still surviving.

Seaman Barker was previously employed with the Callendar Coal Company as a miner, and he joined the Navy in October, 1938. He was the first native of Slamannan to give his life for his country in the present war.

The battleship H.M.S. Royal Oak was sunk, with the loss of 833 members of her crew, as she lay at anchor at the Home Fleet base in Scapa Flow, Orkney, on 14th October.

Falkirk Herald 21st October 1939

DAY OF RAID WARNINGS WIDE AREA TWICE SENT TO COVER
Coast Towns Quiet

Kinghorn and Burntisland received the air-raid warnings, and there also the A.R.P. machine began to function immediately. All precautions were taken, and in Kinghorn the children were marshalled to the shelters, and there spent two hours singing very heartily.

Fifeshire Advertiser
October 21st 1939

PORTRAIT OF A HERO
Glasgow Tramwayman Shot Down Nazi Bomber
Courage is Commended

A few short weeks ago Mr John A Robertson was collecting fares in Glasgow trams. Today his job is to 'collect' German planes and already he has one in the 'bag'. Lance-Bombardier Robertson of an A.A.* battery has been recommended for his

Taking shelter.

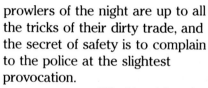

courage in repelling an air attack by German bombers.

* A.A. = Anti-aircraft

Scottish Daily Express
13th November 1939

BLACK-OUT FATALITY

Peeblesshire had its first 'black-out' fatality on Saturday night when Patrick Calvey (41), foreman potato lifter, Brownsland, Biggar, died from injuries received when knocked down by a service bus proceeding towards Peebles. . . He was conveyed to Kello Memorial Hospital, Biggar, where he died an hour later.

Peeblesshire & South Midlothian
Advertiser
17th November 1939

BLACK-OUT REIGN OF TERROR
Women, Children, Stopped by Men

Kirkcaldy women, girls, and children are complaining of being stopped in the street by men during the black-out. . . .

Almost every morning dark tales are going the rounds of uneasy happenings of the night before. The female of the species no longer wants to go out in the evenings alone. Even school children are not safe, for they are being stopped in the dark, and asked to accompany these inhuman specimens. So far the school children have had the sense to run home to their parents . . .

It is evident then that these

prowlers of the night are up to all the tricks of their dirty trade, and the secret of safety is to complain to the police at the slightest provocation.

Fifeshire Advertiser
25th November 1939

ENEMY RAIDERS AGAIN OVER FORTH

Were Nazi aircraft, which flew low over the sea at the mouth of the Firth of Forth early on Thursday morning engaged in mine-laying?

A Fife fisherman said that several aircraft were seen by his mates active some distance away from their vessel. They may have ben enemy machines, he said, as they were 'very like' the German bombers that took part in the raid on October 16.

There appeared to be five machines. Visibility at the time was fairly good, although there were clouds through which the aeroplanes climbed and were lost to view.

Later in the day sharp bursts of machine-gun fire were heard high in the sky over the Forth, off Leven. Previously an unidentified aircraft had been reported in the neighbourhood.

Fighter aircraft on patrol 'spotted' the visitor, and, following a chase in the clouds, the aircraft was identified as a Heinkel, evidently on reconnaissance . . .

Fifeshire Advertiser
2nd December 1939

THE WAR CABINET

Mr Winston Churchill is back in office. As First Lord of the Admiralty, in the newly constituted War Cabinet, he has taken up the position he held at the outset of the last war. . . As First Lord he will bring to the task of getting the last ounce of efficiency out of the Navy those qualities of courage, masterful energy and prevision that he possesses above any other public man of his time.

Aberdeen Bon-Accord and
Northern Pictorial
7th September 1939

MOTHERWELL IN WAR TIME SERVICE FOR ALL

Busy scenes were witnessed on the streets and at the station with the departure of service men. On Sunday similar scenes were witnessed.

In some cases the soldiers were from a distance and were catching train connections at Motherwell. Inquiry was made in some cases for restaurant facilities and it came as rather a disappointment to the visitors when they were informed that all restaurants were closed on Sundays. In the emergency several housewives in the vicinity of the station showed hospitality to the soldiers, providing them with a hot

← Women were quickly recruited to drive public transport when men were called up for the forces

Women workers in a munitions factory

meal and helping them to fill in the time of waiting.

Motherwell Times
8th September 1939

CHILDREN HELP TO FILL SAND-BAGS

Thousands of tons of sand have been excavated this week from Bell's Meadow, and children . . .lent willing assistance in filling sandbags.

Falkirk Herald
9th September 1939

EDITORIAL

The present war will make service demands on women folk to a far greater extent than any previous war has ever done, and

the call for volunteers, . . . will not, we feel sure, go unheeded by the women of Tweeddale. Women in the county have already enrolled in encouraging numbers for civil defence work, but many more are still required. To fill up the gaps enrolment centres are being opened up at four points in the county - at Peebles, Innerleithen, West Linton and Broughton. Peeblesshire women who are willing to undertake work in connection with the evacuation, Civil Nursing, the Land Army, or clerical work, can enrol at these centres. . .

Peeblesshire and South
Midlothian Advertiser
22nd September 1939

WOMEN IN THE WAR
KNITTING IN THE CITY CHAMBERS

I walked in on a pleasant scene the other day at the City Chambers. In a room set aside for the purpose, a large number of ladies sat busily knitting, so busily indeed, that for once tongues were almost silent, and the click of the needles could be clearly heard. The occasion was the opening of the 'Comforts for the Troops' work-party, organised by Mrs Steele, the Lady Provost, who hurried along from another engagement to give the party a happy send-off.

SPHAGNUM MOSS

One of the ways in which those living in the country - and these include the boys and girls evacuated from the towns - can help at the present time is in the collecting of sphagnum moss, which is largely used for hospital dressings. It is getting rather late now for gathering the moss, but if only the weather holds good during the next week or two it should be possible still to obtain a considerable quantity. Several women's organisations in Edinburgh are anxious to get to work to clean the moss and prepare it for use, and some, indeed, have actually started to do so.

Edinburgh Evening News
12th October 1939

Aberdeenshire women knitting comforts for the troops

A.R.P. IN WEST LINTON

Sir,

Permit me to draw your attention to A.R.P. work in West Linton. What do we find? All the good jobs are picked up by a selected few. Men in the observation hut are holding public positions in West Linton. This is grossly unfair to other working men who, would willingly give their services, but are ousted, by men holding salaried positions. . .

Again we find class distinction in the usage of motor cars. Despite the rationing of petrol . . drivers claim priority because they are plastered with A.R.P. notices.

Hitlerism prevails in West Linton. Dictatorship abounds by a few of the 'Mighty'

I am, etc.

SOCIALIST
Peeblesshire & South Midlothian
Advertiser
20th October 1939

CARLOPS DANCE

An enjoyable dance was held in the Village Hall on Saturday night in aid of the Soldiers Fund for cigarettes. The surplus for the fund amounted to £2.

Peeblesshire & South Midlothian Advertiser 27th October 1939

PROVISION FOR WAR HOMELESS

The Public Assistance Officer, as required by the Government, has made provision for food and shelter for persons rendered temporarily homeless and destitute through the destruction of their homes by enemy action and for Government evacuees who leave their new homes and become destitute in neighbouring districts. He has established two stations in the burgh, one at St. Anne's Church Hall, Low Waters and one at St. Cuthbert's Church Hall, Burnbank. A tea urn and 100 cups have been provided free of charge for each station by Hamilton Co-operative Baking Society and by Messrs John Lightbody & Sons. All other necessary arrangements, such as provisions and assistance, have been made.

Hamilton Advertiser 4th November 1993

CONDITIONS IN SOLDIERS' CAMPS
East Stirling M.P.'s Question to War Minister

In the House of Commons on Tuesday, Mr Arthur Woodburn, M.P. for Clackmannan and East Stirlingshire, asked the War Minister if he was aware that young recruits at camps in Scotland were having to send home for additional food and for overcoats, and that hardship was experienced by others without these resources; and would he take steps to see adequate supplies were available.

The Secretary of State said no such complaints had come to his notice. . . He had every reason to believe this was a rumour circulated to shake public confidence.

Falkirk Herald 11th November 1939

A MOTHER'S MESSAGE

Peeblesshire wireless sets were tuned in last Saturday to the short and inspiring address delivered by the Queen. All who heard it must all have been deeply touched and heartened by the Queen's broadcast to the women of the Empire. Men no less than women will note her insistence on the need for carrying on patiently with the normal tasks that all who are not actually serving must fulfil. It is not so difficult to do big things, as the Queen said. But it is often hard to bear the many worries and irritations of war-time life in ordinary homes, and we may be helped in this by remembering that every household feels them to a more or less degree. The Queen herself reminded mothers whose children have been evacuated for safety's sake that she too is parted from her young daughters. In proportion as we can all do our humble part in maintaining our home life and helping in the national effort the victory will be hastened.

Peeblesshire and South Midlothian Advertiser 17th November 1939

THE LION IS RAMPANT GLASGOW AIDS JOCK'S BOX

Everybody in Glasgow was flag-waving for Jock's boxes* - five thousand collectors saw to it. Many members of the public recognised the flag which was handed over in exchange for their donation to provide comforts the Scottish soldiers. It was a replica of the emblem used in the Jock's Box campaign during the last war . . .' For our own brave lands – Hands across the sea'

* 'Jock's boxes' = comforts for the troops.

Glasgow Evening News 25th November 1939

LEVEN MEN WITH FORCES GET THEIR PARCELS

'Good luck and wealth,

Cutting down iron railings for scrap

And the best of health,
And friends who are kind and true,
With heaps of good cheer,
And a Happy New Year-
This is our wish for you.'

This is the 'Greetings from the Leven Red Cross and Scoonie Comforts Fund, Christmas, 1939' card, which has been enclosed in the parcels sent last week to every Leven and Scoonie man serving with H.M. Forces.

A total of 346 parcels has been dispatched. . .

The parcels all contain a cake of shortbread, piece of currant bun, slab of chocolate, packet of cigarettes, a book and one pair of socks.

The parcels which were sent to 'Somewhere in France', contained, in addition, a knitted helmet, scarf, mittens and facecloth...

Fifeshire Advertiser
23rd December 1939

PURGE OF 'REDS' BY TRADE UNIONS

Substantial support is being given by the Trade Union Movement to the campaign of Lord Provost Dollan against Communist influence in local branches of the unions.

This story follows the signing of the Russo-German pact of August 1939

Glasgow Evening News
29th December 1939

FOOD SUPPLIES
Sugar and Tinned Foods in Demand

Since the declaration of war many people have been laying in additional stocks of food, particularly sugar and tinned meats.

Managers of grocery establishments in Falkirk agree that they cannot remember a busier time. So great has been the demand for sugar, in particular, that many shops have placed a restriction on the amount that may be bought by any one customer. The opinion is that present demand will not be maintained, but that the public are simply laying in stores before rationing of foodstuffs is imposed. There is no danger of supplies giving out, even in the face of the present heavy demands.

Falkirk Herald
9th September 1939

WILLING RESPONSE TO APPEAL FOR HELP IN FARM WORK

Many offers have been received in response to the appeal made through the National Farmers' Union for volunteers to help with harvest work in the North-east.

City men, schoolboys, retired farmers and teachers are among those who, from many walks of life, have signified their willingness to work on the land until the crops are secured.

A big list of volunteers has been prepared by Mr T.M. Newbigging, solicitor, secretary of the Aberdeen, Banff and Kincardine Area Executive of the National Farmers' Union.

'I have not had a big demand from farmers so far; but there is sure to be a rush for men when the leading of the grain crop is in full swing.' . . .

'Farmers are already expressing the hope that I shall be able to supply a large number of workers for potato lifting.'

A number of women have come forward with offers to help with farm work. Some of them are willing to tackle either indoor or outdoor tasks.

A typical example was a woman school teacher who handed in her name with the remark: 'If there is any way I can help on a farm I'm willing to try it.'

Aberdeen Weekly Journal
21st September 1939

Women at work in stables

FOOD RATIONING EXPECTED THIS MONTH
TEA NOT AFFECTED AT START
EXTRA SUPPLIES OF MARGARINE

It is expected that food rationing will be established about the end of this month. It will apply to butter, margarine, cooking fats, sugar, meat, bacon and ham. There will be no rationing of tea-at any rate at first.

There will be extra supplies of margarine which, it is hoped, will make up for rather diminished supplies of butter, much of which comes across the North Sea. . . .

All rationing will be on a weight basis, with the exception of meat, which will be fixed at a certain value, so that people may spend their money as they wish. A child will not be allowed as much meat as an adult. Special arrangements will be made for people in hotels or hostels, and a meat meal at any restaurant may mean the surrender of half a coupon.

Dalkeith Advertiser
12th October 1939

DAYLIGHT SAVING
Farm Workers' Hours in the Lothians

At a meeting of the Mid and West Lothian Area Executive Committee of the National Farmers' Union and Chamber of Agriculture of Scotland, held in the Corn Exchange, Gorgie, Edinburgh, yesterday, it was agreed to recommend that owing to the continued operation of the Daylight Saving Bill farm workers should begin work half an hour later in the morning and finish that time later at night, in order that farm work be carried out in daylight.

Edinburgh Evening News
12th October 1939

PENICUIK ALLOTMENTS

The Town Council is arranging a scheme of allotments and is asking for names of people who are willing to work them. It is felt that, as in the last war, a good deal can be done to increase the food supply by this means.

Peeblesshire & South Midlothian
Advertiser 27th October 1939

ADVERTISEMENTS
TRACTORS FOR PLOUGHING UP GRASSLAND

The Agricultural Executive Committee for Peebles and Selkirk are anxious to ascertain what Tractors and Implements are required to deal with the large increase in Ploughing which it is hoped will be obtained this winter.

It is desired that Farmers will make the fullest use of Tractors etc., in their own possession. Where Farmers, however have no means of undertaking ploughing themselves, they are advised to attempt to secure help from neighbouring farmers or make arrangements with local contractors to carry out the work.

GROUND TO FEU

Lady offers part of her Garden Free for the Growing of Vegetables. Apply 598 Advertiser Office, Peebles.

Peeblesshire & South Midlothian
Advertiser 27th October 1939

KIRKCALDY CALLED TO DIG FOR VICTORY
Every Little Patch Can Help The Work

'Dig for Victory' is the new slogan in Kirkcaldy - and you can all do your bit. The Government has recently inaugurated a scheme whereby as much land as possible may be used for the cultivation of garden produce. In Kirkcaldy a Committee has been set up consisting of eight Councillors and three other members representing allotment holders. Their job is to encourage allotment holding - and your job is to respond to the encouragement and cultivate garden produce.

By growing his or her own cabbages, lettuces, sprouts, turnips, beetroot, potatoes, etc., each allotment holder is contributing in no small way in helping this country to gain a quicker and surer victory.

It's up to you to 'dig for victory'. Don't hesitate - get an allotment . . .

Fifeshire Advertiser
23rd December 1939

A new role for women – laying railway track near Cathcart.

'Children are introduced to their cultural heritage and are helped to compare and contrast their life with that of people in other times. They begin to understand some of the ways in which the past can be reconstructed through the use of source material and to appreciate the importance of evidence and its use in making judgements about events.'

Learning and Teaching: The Environment and the Primary School Curriculum. Scottish Education Department. 1984

'Historians employ a range of skills which help to define their discipline:

Using and analysing a range of source materials. Pupils should be helped to analyse both primary evidence and secondary accounts and to detect, in particular, omissions, the personal standpoint of past writers and the use of emotive or figurative language...'

History from 5 to 16. Curriculum Matters No. 11. Department of Education and Science. 1988

The above quotations demonstrate the importance of source material in pupils involvement with what has been called exploration of their past environment. Use of historical sources was traditionally regarded as an activity conducted at a relatively high level, demanding both advanced inferential skills and the necessity to place what was inferred in the context of previous knowledge and understanding.

Of late however, good language teaching, including such activities as cloze procedure and prediction exercises, combined with an ever increasing sophistication in thematic studies at upper primary and secondary level, have enabled the explanation (and subsequent communication) of 'first hand' texts to take their place alongside observation and recording in an active methodology. To provide a country-wide collection of newspaper sources, focussed on a particular year of considerable interest, and capable of producing a range of responses at individual and group level, is a major purpose of this book.

The responses to these glimpses of fifty years ago will vary. Each of the sections in itself could form part of the evidence for an in-depth era study, or it could add a 'Scottish Dimension' to an examination of Britain at war, or it could simply furnish the material for a dramatic presentation 'Our Town in 1939'. A more complete list of suggested responses is appended.

SOME ACTIVITIES

1.FINDING THE MAIN IDEA, or identification of specific themes or main ideas which appear throughout the extracts.
Options for activities in this area include group discussion designed to reach a consensus on what the main idea consists of, headline writing, (or alternatively, where a headline is provided, discussion on appropriateness), prediction exercises, general discussion of issues such as Propaganda (Are there examples in the book? What were the reasons given? Do you think they were justified?)

2. COMPARISON/CONTRAST Pupils could examine features of life in 1939 and draw comparisons and contrasts with the contemporary scene. A range of possibilities presents itself such as improvised or scripted dramatisations of situations then and now: e.g.
Shopping and Food
Conscientious Objectors (and Peace People)
Middle and Working class attitudes (evacuees)
Government and Local Council regulations
Schools and schooling
At work
The role of Women

3. LOCAL STUDIES
(a) Fieldwork
Some activities could be connected with 2 above, viz.

Recruits for the Home Guard drilling with walking sticks and broom handles.

investigating the present condition of places mentioned in the text, making direct comparisons with the written description, or with old photographs and maps (where possible), producing videotapes or slide/tape presentations of findings.

(b) Making particular use of Human Resources
With luck, tracing individuals mentioned in the text, or their descendants. Collecting reminiscences and interviewing, making attempts to discover different perspectives on events; all are possibilities.

(c) Making general use of Human Resources
As above, talking to and obtaining information from members of generations who lived through the prewar years. Interviews could select different aspects of the text and raise questions like 'Was it really like this?'

4. SOURCE MATERIAL AS CREATIVE STIMULUS
(a) Art
There are many opportunities for imaginative art work e.g. 'In the Shelter', 'The First Bombing Raid'; posters; frieze work; appreciation of War Artists (Clydebank Blitz, Greenock shipyards
(b) Drama
(c) Music
(d) Use of contemporary objects and artefacts (Touch and Feel).

Ronald Armstrong

Hitler will send no warning –
so always carry your gas mask